How to Stop Being a

Narcissist

WORKBOOK

Proven Strategies for Overcoming Narcissistic/Manipulative Behavior, Healing Relationships, and Embracing Personal Growth

Harper Evergreen

Disclaimer: The information and exercises provided in this workbook are intended for educational and self-improvement purposes only. The author and publisher are not responsible for any actions taken based on the content of this workbook. Readers are advised to consult with a qualified professional for personalized advice and guidance.

Table of Contents

Introduction

In a world often consumed by self-interest and personal gain, it is a rare and courageous soul who dares to embark on a journey of self-discovery and transformation. It takes immense strength to face the mirror, to peer into the depths of one's own reflection, and to confront the unsettling truth of narcissistic tendencies.

Welcome to a realm of possibility, where the winds of change whisper their secrets and the pages of your story await an extraordinary rewrite. This workbook, "How to Stop Being a Narcissist: Real and Proven Strategies to Change Narcissistic/Manipulative Behavior and Stop Sabotaging Your Relationships," is your compass, your guiding light amidst the storm.

Imagine a life unburdened by the shackles of self-centeredness, a life where empathy and compassion flow freely through the rivers of your being. Envision relationships infused with trust, authenticity, and mutual respect, where love blooms in the fertile soil of self-awareness and growth. This workbook holds the key to unlock the door to that very reality.

In these pages, you will embark on a voyage of self-discovery, unraveling the intricate tapestry of your narcissistic tendencies with unwavering curiosity and determination. Together, we will delve into the depths of your past, seeking to understand the roots from which these patterns sprouted. We will shine a light on the wounds that shaped your worldview, illuminating the path to healing and transformation.

Prepare to confront the echoes of your inner child, embrace vulnerability as a sacred gift, and cultivate the fertile soil of self-compassion. With each turn of the page, you will gain insights into the powerful dynamics of empathy and emotional intelligence, learning to wield them as mighty tools in the art of connection and understanding.

This powerful journey is not for the faint of heart. It requires courage, resilience, and unwavering commitment. But fear not, for within these very words lies the roadmap to liberation. As you navigate through the exercises and assessments, you will find yourself empowered to challenge distorted beliefs, to take accountability for your actions, and to establish healthy boundaries.

This is your invitation to step into a realm of authenticity, where the masks fall away, and the true essence of your being radiates with vibrant brilliance. You possess the power to shape your destiny, nurture relationships that flourish, and sow seeds of change that will reverberate far beyond the boundaries of your own existence.

Dear traveler, embrace this opportunity to transform, to transcend the limitations of your former self. Unleash the warrior within and let the battle cry of change resonate through your very core. The world awaits the emergence of your truest, most authentic self.

Together, let us embark on this odyssey of personal growth, as we unlock the mysteries of narcissistic tendencies and ignite the flame of transformation. The time has come to stop being a narcissist and to step into the realm of profound connection, love, and meaningful relationships.

The journey begins now. Are you ready to claim your destiny?

Chapter 1: Recognizing Narcissistic Traits

Identifying Narcissistic Behavior:

- Reflect on a recent situation where your narcissistic behavior negatively affected a relationship. How did it make you feel? How do you envision your ideal self in relationships?

- Rate your level of commitment to personal growth and change on a scale of 1-10. What motivates you to break free from narcissistic patterns?

_____

_____

_____

_____

_____

_____

- Self-Reflection Exercise: Describe a recent situation where you exhibited narcissistic behavior. How did your actions or attitudes demonstrate self-centeredness or disregard for others?

_____

_____

_____

_____

_____

- Behavioral Observation: Take note of three instances this week where you noticed narcissistic tendencies in your behavior. Reflect on the triggers and emotions associated with those behaviors.

The Narcissistic Spectrum:

Complete the following structured questionnaire to evaluate the intensity of narcissistic traits you exhibit. Reflect on the results and consider the impact of these traits on your relationships.

Self-Assessment Quiz: Evaluating Narcissistic Traits

Instructions: Please read each statement carefully and select the response that best represents your thoughts, feelings, and behaviors. As you respond to each question, be sincere with yourself. Reflect on the results and consider the impact of these traits on your relationships.

1. I have an inflated sense of self-importance and believe that I am special or unique.

   a) Very infrequently or never

   b) Occasionally

c) Sometimes

d) Frequently

2. I have a constant need for admiration and attention from others.

a) Very infrequently or never

b) Occasionally

c) Sometimes

d) Frequently

3. I have a strong sense of entitlement and believe that I deserve special treatment.

a) Very infrequently or never

b) Occasionally

c) Sometimes

d) Frequently

4. I tend to exploit or take advantage of others to achieve my own goals.

a) Very infrequently or never

b) Occasionally

c) Sometimes

d) Frequently

5. I lack empathy and struggle to understand or care about others' feelings.

a) Very infrequently or never

b) Occasionally

c) Sometimes

d) Frequently

6. I often envy others and feel a sense of superiority over them.

a) Very infrequently or never

b) Occasionally

c) Sometimes

d) Frequently

7. I require constant praise and recognition to maintain my self-esteem.

   a) Very infrequently or never

   b) Occasionally

   c) Sometimes

   d) Frequently

8. I have a tendency to manipulate or exploit others to get what I want.

   a) Very infrequently or never

   b) Occasionally

   c) Sometimes

   d) Frequently

9. I struggle to handle criticism and often react defensively or with anger.

   a) Very infrequently or never

   b) Occasionally

   c) Sometimes

d) Frequently

10. I find it difficult to maintain healthy and fulfilling long-term relationships.

a) Very infrequently or never

b) Occasionally

c) Sometimes

d) Frequently

Scoring: Score each response by giving it one of the following values:

- Very infrequently or never: 1 point

- Occasionally: 2 points

- Sometimes: 3 points

- Frequently: 4 points

Add up your scores for all the questions to calculate your total score.

Interpreting Your Results:

- 10-16 points: Your narcissistic traits are minimal, and they have a limited impact on your relationships.

- 17-24 points: You exhibit some narcissistic traits occasionally, which may affect your relationships to some extent.

- 25-32 points: Your narcissistic traits are moderate, and they can have a noticeable impact on your relationships.

- 33-40 points: You exhibit narcissistic traits frequently, and they significantly impact your relationships.

Reflect on your total score and consider how these traits may be affecting your interactions with others. Remember that this self-assessment quiz provides a general indication and is not a substitute for professional diagnosis or guidance. If you have concerns about your narcissistic traits or their impact on your relationships, consider seeking support from a qualified therapist or counselor.

- Reflect on a situation where you witnessed someone else's narcissistic behavior. How did it affect you and your perception of that person?

_____

_____

_____

_____

_____

_____

_____

_____

_____

_____

_____

Self-Reflection Exercises:

- Writing Prompts: Describe a situation where you felt the need for constant admiration or validation from others. How did this behavior impact your relationships?

_____

_____

_____

_____

_____

_____

_____

_____

_____

_____

_____

- Values and Empathy Exercise: List three values that are important to you. Reflect on how these values align or conflict with empathetic behavior.

_____

_____

_____

_____

_____

_____

_____

_____

_____

_____

_____

_____

_____

_____

_____

_____

_____

_____

_____

Chapter 2: Understanding the Root Causes

Exploring Childhood Experiences:

- Guided Visualization: Close your eyes and imagine a significant event from your childhood that may have contributed to the development of narcissistic tendencies. Write about it and reflect on its impact.

_____

_____

_____

_____

_____

_____

_____

_____

_____

- Reflect on any childhood experiences where you felt unseen, unheard, or invalidated. How might these experiences relate to your current narcissistic behaviors?

Emotional Wounds and Insecurities:

- Emotional Inventory: Identify three emotional wounds or insecurities that contribute to your narcissistic behavior. How do these wounds manifest in your interactions with others?

_____

_____

_____

_____

_____

_____

_____

_____

_____

_____

_____

- Healing Activities: Choose one healing practice (journaling, meditation, therapy, etc.) to engage in regularly to address unresolved emotional wounds.

Therapeutic Approaches:

- Inner Child Work Exercise: Visualize yourself as a child and write a compassionate letter to your inner child, acknowledging their needs and offering support and understanding.

- Research different therapeutic approaches such as cognitive-behavioral therapy (CBT) or psychodynamic therapy. Reflect on which approach might be most helpful for you and consider seeking professional help if needed.

Chapter 3: Building Empathy and Emotional Intelligence

Developing Empathy

- Perspective-Taking Exercise: Choose a situation where you disagreed with someone. Write a short paragraph from their perspective, considering their thoughts, feelings, and experiences.

- Recall a time when someone showed empathy towards you. How did it feel to be understood and validated?

_____

_____

_____

_____

_____

_____

_____

_____

_____

_____

_____

Emotional Regulation:

- Emotional Awareness Practice: Pay attention to your emotions throughout the day. Notice and label them, and reflect on their triggers and any patterns you observe.

_____

_____

_____

_____

_____

_____

_____

_____

_____

_____

_____

- Identify three healthy ways you can regulate and manage intense emotions. Practice using one of these strategies the next time you experience heightened emotions.

_____

Practicing Active Listening:

- Active Listening Role-Play: Enlist a friend or family member to engage in a role-playing exercise where you practice active listening skills such as paraphrasing, reflecting, and clarifying.

- Challenge yourself to practice active listening in one conversation each day this week. Take note of how it affects your understanding and connection with others.

Chapter 4: Cultivating Self-Compassion and Authenticity

Embracing Vulnerability:

- Vulnerability Reflection: Identify a situation where you struggle with vulnerability. Explore the underlying fears or beliefs associated with it. How might embracing vulnerability enhance your relationships?

_____

_____

_____

- Choose one small step towards vulnerability that you can take this week. Write it down and commit to following through with it.

_____

_____

_____

_____

_____

_____

_____

_____

_____

_____

_____

Practicing Self-Compassion:

- Self-Compassion Letter: Write a compassionate letter to yourself, acknowledging your struggles and offering forgiveness and acceptance. Reflect on the emotions that arise during this exercise.

_____

_____

_____

_____

_____

_____

_____

_____

_____

- Develop a list of five self-care activities that nurture your physical, emotional, and mental well-being. Schedule one self-care activity each day for the next week.

_____

_____

_____

_____

_____

_____

Authenticity in Relationships:

- Values Alignment Exercise: Reflect on your core values and assess how well your current behaviors in relationships align with those values. Identify one action you can take to live more authentically according to your values.

- Engage in a conversation with a trusted friend or partner where you openly express your true thoughts and feelings. Reflect on how it felt to be authentic in that interaction.

Chapter 5: Transforming Narcissistic Behaviors

Challenging Distorted Beliefs:

- Cognitive Restructuring: Identify one negative belief or cognitive distortion related to narcissistic behavior. Challenge and reframe that belief with a more balanced and realistic thought.

_____

_____

_____

_____

- Create three positive affirmations that counteract negative self-perceptions. Repeat them daily and notice any shifts in your self-perception and behavior.

_____

_____

_____

Accountability and Responsibility:

- Behavior Tracking: Keep a record for one week of instances where you demonstrated accountability and responsibility. Reflect on the positive outcomes and the impact on your relationships.

- Think of a specific situation where you have hurt someone. Write a sincere apology and identify appropriate restitution to make amends.

Healthy Boundaries:

- Boundary Exploration: Reflect on your boundaries in relationships. Are they too rigid or too permeable? Identify one boundary you can establish or reinforce to promote healthier dynamics.

- Engage in a role-playing exercise where you practice setting and maintaining healthy boundaries in different relationship scenarios.

Chapter 6: Nurturing Healthy Relationships

Communication Skills:

- Assertiveness Training: Practice assertive communication techniques, such as using "I" statements, active listening, and expressing needs and boundaries clearly.

- Engage in a role-playing exercise where you simulate a conflict scenario and practice resolving it through constructive communication and compromise.

Empowering Others:

- Recognition and Appreciation Exercise: Identify three strengths or contributions of someone in your life. Express genuine appreciation and recognition for those qualities.

_____

_____

_____

_____

_____

_____

_____

_____

_____

_____

_____

_____

- Delegate a task or responsibility to someone, allowing them to contribute and grow. Reflect on the experience and the impact it had on your relationship.

_____

_____

_____

_____

_____

Building Mutual Trust:

- Rebuilding Trust Exercise: Identify a relationship where trust has been damaged. Create a plan outlining consistent actions, open communication, and transparency to rebuild trust.

_____

_____

_____

_____

_____

- Engage in trust-building activities such as team-building exercises or collaborative projects. Reflect on how these activities contribute to fostering trust in relationships.

_____

_____

_____

_____

_____

_____

_____

_____

_____

_____

Conclusion

As we reach the final pages of this transformative journey, take a moment to honor the depth of your courage, resilience, and commitment. You have traversed the intricate labyrinth of narcissistic tendencies, peeling back the layers of self-deception to reveal the radiant truth that lies within.

Throughout this book, you have immersed yourself in self-reflection, engaged in thought-provoking exercises, and confronted the shadows that once held you captive. You have embarked on a path of healing, growth, and personal transformation, and for that, you deserve commendation.

But remember, dear traveler, this is not the end, but merely the beginning of a lifelong pursuit of self-awareness and authentic connection. The insights gained and strategies learned within these pages are meant to be integrated into the very fabric of your being, woven into the tapestry of your existence.

As you reflect upon your journey, celebrate the progress you have made. Notice how your relationships have begun to blossom with newfound empathy, compassion, and authenticity. Revel in the profound connection that arises when you let go of the shackles of self-centeredness and embrace the boundless potential of true partnership.

But also recognize that this path is not without its challenges. There may be times when old patterns resurface, tempting you to slip back into familiar ways. It is in these moments that you must summon the strength and wisdom you have cultivated. Remind yourself of the remarkable transformation you have undergone and recommit to the principles that guide you towards a more fulfilling and fulfilling life.

Remember, too, that personal growth is a continuous process. Each day presents an opportunity to deepen your understanding, refine your behaviors, and nurture the seeds of change that have been planted within you. Embrace the lessons you have learned and carry them with you as you navigate the ever-evolving landscape of your relationships.

In closing, know that you are not alone. Countless others have walked this path before you, and many more will follow. Reach out for support when needed, lean on trusted friends or seek guidance from professionals who can provide the insights and tools to support your ongoing growth.

May this book serve as a guiding light on your journey, illuminating the way towards a life enriched by genuine connection, profound self-awareness, and authentic love. You possess the power to transcend the limitations of your former self and step into a reality where empathy, kindness, and meaningful relationships flourish.

The world awaits the full expression of your transformed being. Embrace the gift of change and embark on the adventure that lies ahead. You have the power to stop being a narcissist and embark on a remarkable journey of self-discovery, healing, and love.

With profound admiration for your unwavering commitment to growth, we bid you farewell on this chapter of your odyssey. May your path be illuminated by the radiance of your true self, forever shining brightly upon the world.

Safe travels, dear seeker, as you continue to navigate the infinite possibilities that await.

Note: The exercises and assessments in this workbook are designed to promote self-reflection and personal growth. For severe cases of narcissism or when therapy is required, it is important to seek professional guidance from qualified therapists or counselors.

*** The End ***

Made in the USA
Las Vegas, NV
29 September 2024

95946765R00031